D1714217

CELEBRITY BIOS

Reese Witherspoon

Ursula Rivera

HIGH
interest
books

Children's Press®
A Division of Scholastic Inc.
New York / Toronto / London / Auckland / Sydney
Mexico City / New Delhi / Hong Kong
Danbury, Connecticut

Dedicated to Reese's biggest Fr

Book Design: Michael DeLisio
Contributing Editor: Shira Laskin

Photo Credits: Cover © Lisa Rose/Globe Photos, Inc.; pp. 4, 18 © Fitzroy Barrett/Globe Photos, Inc.; pp. 7, 10, 12, 15, 16, 21, 28, 33, 34 © Everett Collection, Inc.; p. 8 ©Rangefinders/Globe Photos, Inc.; p. 9 © Howard Jacqueline/Corbis Sygma; p. 25 © ES/Globe Photos, Inc.; p. 26 © Globe Photos, Inc.; p. 30 © Sonia Moskowitz/Globe Photos, Inc.; p. 37 © Nina Prommer/Globe Photos, Inc.; p. 39 © Scott Weiner/Globe Photos, Inc.

Library of Congress Cataloging-in-Publication Data

Rivera, Ursula.
    Reese Witherspoon / Ursula Rivera.
    p. cm.—(Celebrity bios)
    Summary: Chronicles the childhood, marriage and family life, and acting career of the star of films such as *Election, Pleasantville,* and *Legally Blonde.*
    Includes index.
    ISBN 0-516-24337-3 (lib. bdg.)—ISBN 0-516-27860-6 (pbk.)
    1. Witherspoon, Reese, 1976—Juvenile literature. 2. Motion picture actors and actresses—United States—Biography—Juvenile literature. [1. Witherspoon, Reese, 1976- 2. Actors and actresses. 3. Women—Biography.] I. Title. II. Series.

PN2287.W54R58 2003
791.43'028'092—dc21

                                        2003000853

CONTENTS

CHAPTER ONE

Brains and Beauty

"I've always been very serious about what I do. I know what I want out of life, and I try to focus on those things."

—*Reese in an interview with* E! Online

She's a busy mother, a Hollywood wife, and a box-office superstar. As an intelligent, educated woman, Reese Witherspoon is all these things and more. Her performances in films such as *Election* and *Pleasantville* have made her a favorite with movie critics. Reese has charmed audiences in *Legally Blonde* and *Sweet Home Alabama*. Reese is also the mother of an active

As a leading lady with a loving family, Reese has *plenty* to smile about.

daughter, Ava Elizabeth. To top it off, Reese's husband, Ryan Phillippe, is of one the hottest young stars in Hollywood! Where did superstar actress, wife, and mother, Reese Witherspoon, get her start?

SOUTHERN BELLE

Laura Jean Reese Witherspoon was born in New Orleans, Louisiana, on March 22, 1976. She was raised in Nashville, Tennessee. Her father, John, is a surgeon and her mother, Betty, is a professor of nursing. Reese has an older brother named John. Reese has described members of her family as "very eccentric," yet she is very close to her parents and brother.

Reese attended a private girls' school in Nashville called Harpeth Hall. She was a good student who thought she would grow up to become a doctor or nurse, like her parents. Reese was expected to be well behaved and to have good manners. She even attended etiquette classes!

When Reese was seven years old she performed in a commercial for a local Nashville flower shop. She also began modeling. Reese loved acting, but didn't think it would be her career. "I had no aspirations of being an actress," she told the *Calgary Sun.* "I just accepted that I would be a doctor of some sort." Within a few years, though, Reese found herself auditioning for a major motion picture.

EARLY SUCCESS

In 1991, at fourteen years old, Reese went with some friends to audition for a feature film, *The Man in the Moon.* She hoped to get work as an extra. An extra plays a small role with a few lines to speak. Instead, Reese got the lead part!

Even as a young actress, Reese was determined to do her best.

Reese traveled very far to play Nonnie Parker in *A Far Off Place.* She had to take a two-day flight from the United States to Africa, where the movie was filmed.

The cast included actors Sam Waterston, from TV's *Law and Order,* and Tess Harper. Robert Mulligan, director of the 1962 film, *To Kill A Mockingbird,* directed the movie.

Reese received rave reviews for her appearance in *The Man in the Moon.* "Fresh-faced and exuberant," one critic called her, while others said that Reese's work in the film was "magical." Reese began to get other offers to act in films. That same year, actor-director Diane Keaton invited Reese to play a part in the Lifetime TV movie, *Wildflower.* Again, Reese impressed critics with her performance.

In 1993, Reese was chosen to star in Disney's *A Far Off Place.* Reese traveled to Africa to film the movie. She played a young girl that had to escape evil elephant hunters in the desert. To learn the African language she spoke in the film, Reese studied with an African tribe. She quickly followed that movie with a role in *Jack the Bear,* starring Danny de Vito. "The camera loves [Reese]" said Marshall Herskovitz, the director of *Jack the Bear.* "She is down to earth … and she has a great dignity about her," he told *People* magazine.

Reese (seated at left) may not have been on screen that much in *Jack the Bear*, but her performance earned her rave reviews.

While playing best friends in the 1996 film, *Fear,* Reese and Alyssa
Milano formed a real-life friendship that lasts to this day.

In 1993 and 1994, Reese continued making
movies with well-known actors and directors.
She was cast in *Return to Lonesome Dove,* a
TV movie starring Barbara Hershey and Jon
Voight. In *S.F.W.,* Reese co-starred with
Stephen Dorff. In 1996 she performed in *Fear*
as a young woman with a psychotic boyfriend,
played by Mark Wahlberg. *Fear* was a huge hit
with teen audiences, and Reese became famil-
iar to moviegoers as a result.

Following the success of *Fear,* Reese was
offered roles in a series of teen horror films.

They included *Scream, I Know What You Did Last Summer,* and *Urban Legend.* She turned them all down. "All that screaming … is not fulfilling," she said. Reese wanted to act in different projects that would help her grow as an actress. She didn't want to feel trapped in one type of role.

Reese's next movie may not have been a teen horror film, but it was a dark and difficult part. In *Freeway,* Reese played Vanessa, a tough, young girl with family problems. Vanessa gets

Did You Know?

The Witherspoon family has an important connection to American history. One of Reese's ancestors, John Witherspoon, signed the Declaration of Independence. He was also the president of Princeton University from 1768 to 1774.

dangerously involved with a killer, played by Kiefer Sutherland. The role required Reese to rethink her approach to acting. She had to understand how Vanessa's mind worked. "Before *Freeway* I hadn't done a lot of character work," she told *Entertainment Weekly.* "When I read that script I thought, this scares...me, so I should probably do it. That's when acting sort of clicked with me." Reese knew that working hard to bring her character to life would help her learn more about the art of acting.

Reese's decision to work harder on her character development paid off in a big way. In the *Chicago Sun-Times,* critic Roger Ebert wrote: "Witherspoon is as focused...as a young Jodie Foster." That was quite a compliment. Jodie Foster is a very talented and respected actress. To top it all off, Reese's performance as Vanessa won her the Best Actress Award at the Catalonian Film Festival in Spain!

Playing Vanessa in *Freeway* took Reese on quite a ride. She had to travel through Vanessa's mind to find the best way to bring the character to life.

BACK TO SCHOOL?

While filming movies, Reese was unable to attend high school full-time. Still, she managed to complete her education by doing her homework on the set. As always, Reese remained an excellent student. She graduated on schedule and was accepted to Stanford University in California. Reese loved acting, but still had plans to become a doctor! It felt natural to follow in her parents' footsteps and she wasn't sure that acting was the right path for her.

Reese entered Stanford as a pre-med major, and also spent much of her time reading and studying English literature. She enjoyed her classes, but soon more offers to act in movies were sent her way. Reese knew she had a difficult decision to make: Should she devote herself to acting and put school on hold?

After one full semester at Stanford, Reese received a call from director Robert Benton that helped her make up her mind. He wanted her to

Reese continued her climb to the top opposite Paul Newman in 1998's *Twilight.*

perform in *Twilight,* a film starring Paul Newman and Susan Sarandon. Reese was thrilled. She was being asked to work with very respected actors. She took the part. "I was too busy having a career to go to school," she later realized. Although *Twilight* was not a great success, it helped Reese move forward as an actress.

Pleasantville was filmed partially in black and white to give the movie a 1950s feel. In those scenes, it was up to the actors to provide colorful performances.

BACK IN TIME

Reese's next big role was in *Pleasantville,* a movie about American life in the 1950s. She played a young woman named Mary Sue Parker. Reese's wardrobe was very different from what she was used to wearing. "Those poodle skirts...are the most hideous fashions imaginable," she told the *Calgary Sun.* Reese may not have liked the costumes, but she looked great and performed wonderfully. *Pleasantville* received good reviews from critics and performed strongly at the box office.

Reese had a big year in 1997. In addition to filming *Pleasantville*, it was the year she turned twenty-one years old. She decided to throw herself a birthday party to celebrate. One of Reese's guests brought along his friend, actor Ryan Phillippe. Ryan and Reese sat and talked through the whole party.

Ryan and Reese hit it off immediately. They knew they wanted to spend more time together. Unfortunately, Ryan was leaving the next morning. He was flying to North Carolina to film *I Know What You Did Last Summer*—a movie that Reese had turned down! During Ryan's five-month shoot, he and Reese spoke on the phone and wrote a lot of letters to each other. When the movie was finished, they finally had their first real date.

CHAPTER TWO

Movie Star Mama

"[Reese is] incredibly strong and fiercely independent."

—*Ryan Phillippe in an interview with the* **Calgary Sun**

Reese's love life was on the upswing. By early 1998, she and Ryan Phillippe were very serious about each other. Reese was having a blast in her personal life, and her career was taking off as well.

Reese and Ryan have a quiet family life most of the time. However, when they're in the spotlight, they know how to shine!

DARLING OF THE CRITICS

Reese continued to make movies that were hits with teen audiences. Even when critics gave one of her films a bad review, they often singled her out for compliments. Reese was not quite a box-office superstar—yet. She wasn't known as someone who could "open a movie," like Julia Roberts. Reese continued working steadily, keeping her eye out for good scripts.

In 1999, Reese appeared as Tracy Flick in *Election. Election* was the story of an overachieving high school student who runs for class president. Reese played Tracy as a perky know-it-all who always gets what she wants. Tracy's teacher, Jim McAllister, played by Matthew Broderick, encourages another student to run against her. McAllister must then deal with Tracy's anger. Reese's chemistry with Broderick was fantastic and the critics loved her. "What a fun, fierce actress she is!" the *San Francisco Chronicle* wrote.

Reese did her homework before playing Tracy Flick in *Election*. Reese spent two weeks pretending to be a transfer student at a high school in Nebraska.

Election was produced by MTV Films. Before this movie, MTV was known for making films with little or no moral message behind their stories. With *Election,* however, MTV Films gained respect among critics and audiences. This movie explored the deep, and sometimes dark, relationships that can exist in high school. The film is a comedy, yet it still managed to tell an important story about life.

Reese took her role in *Election* very seriously. She concentrated on how her character would think. Critics loved what they saw. They raved about Reese's facial expressions in the film. In fact, *Film.com* reported that Reese's performance was one of the best female roles of 1999! Reese was thrilled, and even more excitement waited for her just around the corner.

LOVE THAT LASTS

One morning in early 1999, Ryan cooked Reese's favorite breakfast: waffles with strawberries and cream. While Reese ate, Ryan proposed to her! Reese said yes. The couple was married on June 5, 1999. Reese has said of Ryan, "I'm lucky to find a person to share my life, and the best friend I'll ever have." The two young stars are happily married. They have a beautiful daughter, Ava Elizabeth.

Did You Know?

Ryan and Reese got married in South Carolina at the Wide Awake Plantation. They chose the spot because it is the halfway mark between Ryan's family in Delaware and Reese's family in Tennessee.

Although Reese's personal life was keeping her on the go, she kept up the fast pace of her career, too. In 1999, she appeared in *Best Laid Plans* with Josh Brolin. In 2000, Reese played an angel opposite Adam Sandler in *Little Nicky*. She took these small roles in order to balance her busy working life with her family life.

BLONDE BOMBSHELL

Before Ava was born, Reese was asked to play the lead role of Elle Woods in the comedy *Legally Blonde*. In the movie, Elle's boyfriend leaves her because his family doesn't think she is intelligent enough for him. To win him back and prove how smart she is, Elle registers at Harvard Law School and becomes a lawyer. Reese read the script and loved it. She agreed to make the film after her baby was born.

Legally Blonde began filming in the fall of 2000. Reese was faced with the challenges of being a new mother and working at the same time. To help out, Ryan stayed home with Ava a great deal. "[Ryan] was there to take care of me and Ava," Reese said.

When *Legally Blonde* was released during the summer of 2001, it surprised a lot of people. Some critics hated the movie, claiming it wasn't funny enough. Others had a different opinion. Film critic Roger Ebert called the

While playing Elle Woods in *Legally Blonde,* Reese had forty-two wardrobe changes and thirty different hairstyles. Lucky for her she only had one hair *color* to worry about!

movie "impossible to dislike." *People* magazine called it "a feel-good, girl-power comedy." Audiences and critics agreed that Reese was talented, beautiful, and very funny. *Legally Blonde* cost $18 million to make but it made $20 million on its opening weekend alone! Within a few months the movie made more than $90 million dollars.

OPPORTUNITIES EVERYWHERE

The success of *Legally Blonde* gave Reese plenty to be happy about. Her salary grew to about $5 million for each role she played. Reese was also able to create her own production company, called Type A Films. The company focuses on creating film projects that Reese can act in or produce.

The first project Type A began working on was a film version of one of Reese's favorite books, *The Girls' Guide to Hunting and Fishing*, by Melissa Bank. Many other offers

Reese isn't just a movie star mama—she's tried her hand at television, too. In February 2000, Reese guest-starred on two episodes of the hit comedy *Friends*. Here, she is pictured in a scene with David Schwimmer.

came her way, but Reese took her time choosing which ones she liked. In 2001, she began filming *The Importance of Being Earnest,* based on the play by Oscar Wilde. Reese's costars were British actors Colin Firth, Rupert Everett, and Academy Award-winner Judi Dench.

Reese had to learn an English accent for her role in *The Importance of Being Earnest.* She was the only American in the cast and she was very nervous. "I spent six weeks, three hours a day, working on my accent. I was terrified!" she said. Although the cast worked very hard, the film did not do well at the box office. American audiences weren't interested in an old-style comedy. Still, the movie was a great experience for Reese. She was able to meet the challenge of learning to speak with an accent and enjoyed acting in a different style.

When *The Importance of Being Earnest* did not do well at the box office, Reese learned the importance of letting her hard work be its own reward.

CHAPTER THREE

Big Box Office

"I'm never going to be the thinnest girl in Hollywood, or the smartest, or the funniest, or the richest. You have to let go of that garbage if you're going to get anywhere."

—Reese in an interview with Entertainment Weekly

The success of *Legally Blonde* in the summer of 2001 pushed Reese further into the spotlight. That summer, actress Charlize Theron decided to pull out of a Disney film she was working on called *Sweet Home Alabama*. Disney producers couldn't wait to offer Reese the part! She accepted the role with open arms.

It's hard to believe that such a shining superstar once believed that acting wasn't for her.

BACK TO HER ROOTS

In *Sweet Home Alabama,* Reese played Melanie Carmichael. Melanie is a small-town girl from the South who moves to New York City and becomes a fashion designer. After her boyfriend Andrew, played by Patrick Dempsey, proposes to her, Melanie must fly home to Alabama to face her past. The cast featured many well-known comic actors including television's Candice Bergen and Jean Smart.

Reese enjoyed playing a character from the South. It reminded her of her childhood in Nashville. "I felt really connected to my character, Melanie, because she grows up in the South but moves away from her home environment and becomes successful in a whole new world," Reese said in *Seventeen.* As in *Legally Blonde, Sweet Home Alabama* showcased Reese's talent for comedy. She proved once again that she was a loveable leading lady.

Disney did a lot to promote *Sweet Home Alabama.* Posters appeared everywhere, but

Reese was thrilled to play a part that hit so close to home in *Sweet Home Alabama.*

they did not show scenes from the movie. They simply featured Reese in a black turtleneck and skirt. The producers knew that Reese's smiling face could bring audiences in to see the movie. It was proof of her "star" power. Reese could now open a film.

Even though critics didn't like some aspects of the movie, they had compliments for Reese. *The New York Post* reported, "...Witherspoon is such a delight—her comic timing [is] so good." *Rolling Stone* said she showed "sass and class." Audiences clearly liked what they saw.

Since 2001, Reese has taken on a new role—on the *other* side of the camera. She is now a producer, too. Here, she learns behind-the-scenes skills from the crew on the set of *Sweet Home Alabama.*

Sweet Home Alabama opened on September 23, 2002, and made $35 million on its opening weekend. By December 1, the movie had brought in nearly $125 million!

FLIP SIDE OF FAME

Reese has had a high profile in Hollywood since the opening of *Sweet Home Alabama.* Photographers are always excited to get pictures of Reese and Ava. Reese and Ryan are also noticed whenever they go out in public. Reese is certainly in the spotlight, and has to work hard to keep her life balanced.

Reese and Ryan make an effort to put their family first. They have changed their schedules to adapt to family life. Reese now makes only one movie each year. That way she can spend as much time with Ava as possible. Ryan's career continues to grow as well, but it never gets in the way of his love for his wife and daughter. "No movie is so important that it would be worth sacrificing our family life," he said.

Ryan talked about one of the secrets of his successful marriage to Reese. He said that he and Reese attend couples' therapy to help them work out any issues they face. In an interview with *People,* Reese explained that celebrities often make it seem as if their lives are easier, but they aren't. She said about her marriage, "We're normal people with normal problems." She and Ryan focus on what's really important: taking care of Ava and each other.

THE RETURN OF ELLE

Plans have been set for Reese to return as Elle Woods in 2003 with the opening of *Legally Blonde 2: Red, White, and Blonde.* In the sequel, Elle Woods learns to play politics in Washington, D.C. The film also features comedians Bob Newhart and Sally Field.

In addition to being paid $15 million to star in *Legally Blonde 2,* Reese is also producing the movie. She will work closely with the director to hire actors and approve the script. It's a big responsibility, but Reese has proven that she can handle anything that comes her way.

Did You Know?
Reese and Ryan are huge Frank Sinatra fans. They even named their dog after the singer!

Reese has said, "I want to make my life, not just my job, the best it can be. The rest will work itself out."

STRONG AND SUCCESSFUL

Other projects in Reese's future include the thriller *Whiteout,* and a drama called *Vanity Fair.* In *Whiteout,* Reese plays a U.S. marshal who tracks a killer across Antarctica. *Vanity Fair* is based on a nineteenth-century novel

about a lower-class girl in a high-class world. These films show that Reese continues to choose parts that are both challenging and entertaining.

While she thrives as an actress, Reese's most important focus is her family. She works hard to keep Ava's life as normal as possible. That often means that Reese and Ryan invite friends to their house, rather than going out. Of course, the couple still makes plenty of public appearances. In 2002, they appeared together as presenters at the Academy Awards.

That evening, as Ryan and Reese rehearsed for the awards show, Reese realized how far they had come. "I can't believe I made it this far. I never dreamed it was possible." Reese has proved that all her dreams are possible. As a mother, a wife, and a box-office superstar, she's sure to find nothing but success ahead.

With her strong determination, and the support of her family, Reese can achieve anything she puts her mind to.

TIMELINE

1976	• Laura Jean Reese Witherspoon is born on March 22.
1991	• Reese auditions for *The Man In the Moon* and is cast as the lead.
	• Reese appears in *Wildflower* directed by Diane Keaton.
1993	• Reese travels to Africa to film *A Far Off Place.*
	• Reese appears in *Jack the Bear,* with Danny de Vito.
1994	• Reese costars in with Stephen Dorff in *S.F.W.*
1996	• *Fear* opens, starring Reese, Mark Wahlberg, and Alyssa Milano.
	• Reese plays opposite Kiefer Sutherland in *Freeway.*
1997	• Reese meets Ryan Phillippe at her twenty-first birthday party.
	• Reese attends Stanford University as a pre-med major.
1998	• Reese leaves college and stars in *Twilight* with Paul Newman and Susan Sarandon.
	• *Pleasantville* opens with Reese, Tobey Maguire, and Joan Allen.

TIMELINE

1999	• Reese wins rave reviews as Tracy Flick in *Election*.
	• Reese and Ryan are married on June 5.
2000	• Reese appears with Adam Sandler in *Little Nicky*.
2001	• *Legally Blonde* opens and goes on to make nearly $100 million.
2002	• Reese appears in *The Importance of Being Earnest* with Rupert Everett and Judi Dench.
	• *Sweet Home Alabama* opens and earns more than $125 million.
2003	• *Legally Blonde 2: Red, White, and Blonde* opens.
	• Plans for filming *Whiteout* continue.

FACT SHEET

Name	Laura Jean Reese Witherspoon
Born	March 22, 1976
Birthplace	New Orleans, Louisiana
Family	John Witherspoon, father; Betty Witherspoon, mother; John Witherspoon, brother; Ryan Phillippe, husband; Ava Elizabeth, daughter.
Height	5'2"
Hair	Blonde
Eyes	Blue
Sign	Aries

Favorites

Movie	*Overboard* with Goldie Hawn and Kurt Russell
Musicians	Lauryn Hill and Fiona Apple
Food	Vegetarian
Books	*The Diary of Anne Frank,* by Anne Frank *The Catcher in the Rye,* by J. D. Salinger

NEW WORDS

aspiration (ass-pi-**ray**-shuhn) a strong desire to do something great or important

audition (aw-**dish**-uhn) a short performance by an actor, singer, musician, or dancer to see whether he or she is suitable for a part in a play, concert, etc.

critic (**krit**-ik) someone whose job it is to write a review of a book, movie, play, television program, etc.

dignity (**dig**-nuh-tee) a quality or manner that makes a person worthy of honor or respect

director (duh-**rek**-tur) the person in charge of making a play, a movie, or a radio or television program

eccentric (ek-**sen**-trik) acting odd or strange, but in a harmless or charming way

etiquette (**et**-uh-ket) the rules of polite behavior

hideous (**hid**-ee-uhss) ugly or horrible

perky (**purk**-ee) cheerful

NEW WORDS

producer (pruh-**dooss**-ur) the person in charge of the overall making of a movie

promote (pruh-**mote**) to make the public aware of something

raved (**rayvd**) to have praised something enthusiastically

review (ri-**vyoo**) a piece of writing that gives an opinion of a new movie, book, play, etc.

surgeon (**sur**-juhn) a doctor who performs operations

thriller (**thril**-ur) an exciting story that is filled with action, mystery, or suspense

Glamour Reese Witherspoon
http://www.reese-witherspoon.org
Check out this fan site dedicated to Reese for up-to-the-minute news about her life and career.

The Reese Witherspoon Collection
http://www.geocities.com/hollywood/makeup/1595/
reesewitherspoon.html
Check out this site for in-depth interviews, quotes, and pictures of Reese.

The Internet Movie Database (IMDb)
http://www.imdb.com
This is a great resource for information on the careers of Reese or Ryan and any of their co-stars. Find filmographies, images, and biographies on thousands of stars!

Actress: Reese Witherspoon
http://www.the-movie-times.com/thrsdir/actress/
actressProfiles.mv?rwitherspoon
Visit this site to find out how much each movie made at the box office.

The Original Ryan Phillippe Web page
http://www.ryan-phillippe.com
Now that you know all about Reese, find out more about her husband, Ryan Phillippe, on this site. Read interviews, look at photos, and check out his filmography.

RESOURCES

You can write to Reese at:
Reese Witherspoon
c/o International Creative Management
8942 Wilshire Blvd.
Beverly Hills, CA 90211 USA
Please include a self-addressed, business-sized
(it should be able to hold a standard sized postcard),
stamped envelope.

INDEX

INDEX

About the Author

Ursula Rivera was born and raised in New York City.
She has been writing about celebrities for several years.

3+M

THIS ITEMS VALUE IS $6.95
PLEASE TREAT WITH GREAT CARE